W9-AVN-311

Houses

by the Water

ROCKPORT

Houses
by the Water

ROCKPORT
PUBLISHERS

GLOUCESTER MASSACHUSETTS

Text: Ana Cristina G. Cañizares

Graphic Design & Layout: Emma Termes Parera

Copyright for the international edition:

© H Kliczkowski-Onlybook, S.L.

La Fundición, 15. Polígono Industrial Santa Ana

28529 Rivas-Vaciamadrid, Madrid, Spain

Ph.: +34 91 666 50 01

Fax: +34 91 301 26 83

onlybook@onlybook.com

www.onlybook.com

Copyright for the English language edition:

© 2005 by Rockport Publishers, Inc.

Published in the United States of America by

Rockport Publishers, a member of

Quayside Publishing Group

33 Commercial Street

Gloucester, Massachusetts 01930-5089

Tel.: (978) 282-9590

Fax: (978) 283-2742

www.rockpub.com

Library of Congress Cataloging-in-Publication Data available

ISBN: 1-59253-179-2

10 9 8 7 6 5 4 3 2 1

All rights reserved. No part of this book may be reproduced in any form without
written permission of the copyright owners. All images in this book have been
reproduced with the knowledge and prior consent of the artists concerned, and no
responsibility is accepted by producer, publisher, or printer for any infringement of
copyright or otherwise arising from the contents of this publication. Every effort has
been made to ensure that credits accurately comply with information supplied.

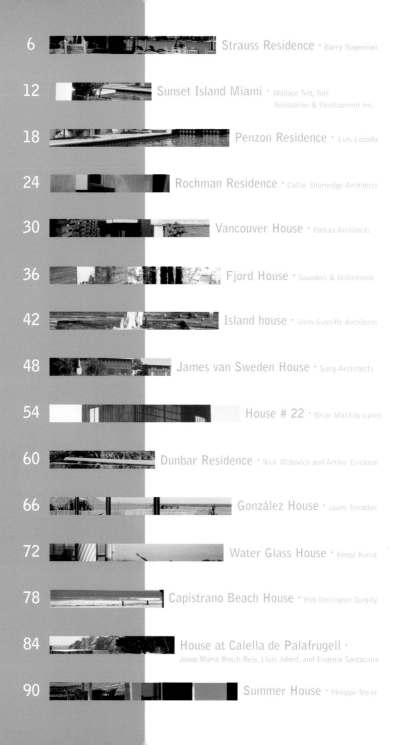

STRAUSS RESIDENCE

Architect: Barry Sugerman
Location: Miami, Florida, United States
Photographs: © Pep Escoda

The Strauss residence is a dream come true for its boating-enthusiast owners, particularly because of the private dock that is conveniently located right in front of the house. All of the rooms in this architecturally typical Florida home face the waterway on which the house is located, affording residents a lovely view from all rooms.

A hallway leads to the kitchen, living room and a dining area where residents gather for meals around a lovely mahogany table. A cozy eating niche that branches off the west side of the hallway looks out over the deck, which is also the venue for barbecues.

SUNSET ISLAND MIAMI

Interior Design Architects: Wallace Tutt, Tutt Renovation & Development Inc.
Location: Miami, Florida, United States
Photographs: © Pep Escoda

When you approach this villa along the beautifully landscaped road leading up to it, you come upon a lovely, well-manicured front yard. Upon entering, a gracefully curving staircase indicates the presence of a second floor, which accommodates the bedrooms and the activities of the private sphere.

Preparing food in the kitchen under its striking round arch is a pure pleasure. A glass door leads out onto a terrace where the nearly juxtaposed swimming pool and sea appear to blend into one another. In the very small area that separates them, residents sunbathe in lounge chairs or hop on a boat moored nearby for a quick, refreshing ride.

PENZON RESIDENCE

Architect: Luis Lozada
Location: Miami, Florida, United States
Photographs: © Pep Escoda

The residents of this Lighthouse Point home were impressed by the work of the Venezuelan architect and designer Luis Lozada, who is also the founder of Architectural Design Form Group Corporation.

The residents asked him to design a series of five decorative objects for their home. In order to ensure that the décor of this 13,800-square-foot (1,288-square-meter) residence would turn out well, Lozada was asked to undertake the required remodeling. The art objects, furniture and fabric, all of which have an African feel, harmonize superbly with the earth tones of the house itself.

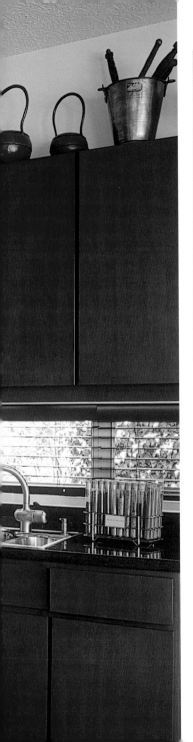

ROCHMAN RESIDENCE

Architect: Callas Shortridge Architects
Location: Pacific Palisades, California, United States
Photographs: © Undine Pröhl

Sitting on the edge of a downhill slope on the hills of the Pacific Palisades, this renovated late 1950s home overlooks the Santa Monica and Malibu coastlines. The initial scheme was conceived by the late Frank Israel, and was developed by his former partners Barbara Callas and Steven Shortridge.

The 3,000-square-foot (279-square-meter) home appears as a single-story building on the street side, yet drops down two stories on the ocean side. Due to height restrictions and setback requirements, the roof was designed as a continuous horizontal parapet shared by exterior walls that lean outward from the core of the house, increasing the interior sense of space.

The open-air dining terrace on the upper level is protected from the sun and heat by a slatted, cantilevered roof.

VANCOUVER HOUSE

Architect: Patkau Architects
Location: Vancouver, British Columbia, Canada
Photographs: © Undine Pröhl

This 3,071-square-foot (285-square-meter) residence looks across English Bay to the North Shore Mountains that dominate the Vancouver skyline. The narrow plot of land, 33 feet (10 meters) wide by 155 feet (47 meters) deep, was limited to 26 feet (8 meters) in width due to required side yard setbacks. The narrow plot of land led the architects to exploit the space vertically and out towards the water, creating a spectacular home in which water is a recurring motif. Distributed over three levels, the house contains a basement level and two floors above ground. A unique perspective of the landscape as well as infinite reflections cast by the pool can be enjoyed from different vantage points on the upper level of the house.

The bedroom, inundated with natural light and endowed with high ceilings, has direct access to the pool and terrace.

FJORD HOUSE

Architect: Saunders & Wilhelmsen
Location: Hardanger Fjord, Norway
Photographs: © Bent Renè Synnevag

A young Canadian/Norwegian firm dedicated to experimental, environmental, and innovative design created this summer cabin set in one of Norway's most beautiful fjords. The architects created an architectural vision in line with their convictions: originality, independence, and respect for the environment. They succeeded in constructing a contemplative space that combines with the natural surroundings in a subtle contrast to the dramatic landscape.

The retreat is divided into two parts: a space designated for eating and sleeping and a smaller general-purpose space. A long and slender outdoor floor links the two rooms and faces the water, giving mesmerizing views of the fjord. newspapers were used as insulation.

This 263-square-foot (24-square-meter) project is divided into two structures. The abstract design opens a dialogue with nature that refreshes its occupants and provides a renewed perspective on life and nature.

ISLAND HOUSE

Architect: Shim-Sutcliffe Architects
Location: St. Lawrence River, Ontario, Canada
Photographs: © James Dow

This summer home, in a meadow that borders the St. Lawrence River, explores the element of water in the form of a man-made pond. The Island House, given its name for the body of water that surrounds the main living area, engages the existing landscape and creates its own. The river establishes a water theme that dominates the overall design of the home.

A long, low concrete wall is set into the sloping terrain that descends towards the river. The plan interlocks two linear flat-roofed rectangular 'bars' around a square living room pavilion. Both low roofs are planted with wild flowers, becoming abstract meadows themselves in a continuation of the surrounding landscape.

JAMES VAN SWEDEN HOUSE

Architect: Sorg Architects
Location: Sherwood, Maryland, United States
Photographs: © Robert Lautman & Steven Ahlgren

In a small, rural town like Sherwood, set against Chesapeake Bay's Ferry Cove, modern architecture is an unexpected sight amidst the farms, antique shops and ice cream parlors. Despite local resistance to Suman Sorg's house for landscape architect James van Sweden, the project has been acclaimed internationally. An unpretentious interpretation of Modernist elegance, it establishes an inspired and cohesive relationship with the surrounding landscape.

Influenced by her childhood in India and her experience as a Peace Corps volunteer, Sorg considers herself an imperfectionist, opting for a rough kind of architecture that benefits from the weathering of time and use.

51

The living room, dining area and bedroom face the bay in an open, loftlike space where furniture and art mix modern and country metaphors in a sensitively designed arrangement of color and form.

HOUSE #22

Architect: Brian MacKay-Lyons
Location: Oxner's Head, Nova Scotia, Canada
Photographs: © Undine Pröhl

A pair of lanternlike buildings floats atop hills that overlook the juncture of the LaHave River and the sea. The main house and guesthouse are aligned on a north-south axis, facing the river or ocean. The natural wetland formed between the two mounds was conceived as a central garden. The mirrored buildings are set 450 feet (137 meters) apart and linked by concrete block walls that lead towards the garden.

Each building has its entry and service elements on the east side of the concrete wall. In the primary space, 8-foot-high (2.4 meters) glazing and horizontal sliding barn doors form the base, while the second floor receives natural light from enveloping glass panels.

A repetitive field of windows punched into the upper portion of the house inundates the interior with natural light. The wooden plinth articulates a long block wall that defines the different functions of the home.

DUNBAR RESIDENCE

Architect: Nick Milkovich and Arthur Erickson
Location: Maui, Hawaii, United States
Photographs: © Ron Dahlquist

Seeming to float among the lava rock formations of the western shores of Maui, this house in Makena is a spectacular vision of ordered civilization amidst nature's chaos. Surrounded by a green expanse of thick vegetation and practically submerged in the waters of the Pacific, the house features stunning views through seamless glass windows and appears shiplike from the ocean.

The three reefs that protect this portion of the shore allowed the architects to place the house very close to the surf. The site, however, required a steep ascent to be able see over the rocks. The main level contains a spacious living room with 11-foot (3.4 meters) high unframed glass walls that slide open to join with the terrace.

GONZÁLEZ HOUSE

Architect: Javier Terrados
Location: Granada, Spain
Photographs: © Fernando Alda

The lot on which this house stands is located near the sea in Los Yesos, a village south of Granada. It is treated as a diaphanous summer house, open to the exterior so that its inhabitants can be outside as often as possible. The clients wanted to evoke and sustain the memory of what had been their summer activity for many years: traveling by trailer.

This idea became the image that directed and molded the project during its design and execution. To take advantage of the slope, they planned an elongated volume perpendicular to the slope, which is closed towards the mountain and open towards the sea.

The rooms have been arranged with both the views and the proximity of the house to the sea in mind. On the side facing the mountain, where the living spaces are more closed, there is an elongated section containing the bathrooms and bedrooms. There is also a point of access at one end of the house.

WATER GLASS HOUSE

Architect: Kengo Kuma
Location: Atami, Japan
Photographs: © Fujitsuka Mitumasa

The main purpose of the Water Glass House is guest accommodation. It has three floors, and occupies half of the area of a 120-square-foot (11-square-meter) plot. It is situated on the Atami coast on the edge of a cliff, facing the Pacific Ocean.

Although in past years, the use of concrete as a construction element is frequent in Japanese architecture, for Kuma it is too heavy and has produced an architecture of monumental form. He has set up the principle of transparency against the use of this material. The materials used are always light, such as glass, steel, or wood; they are materials of the present.

The architecture of Kengo Kuma is an experiment into the possibilities of attaining the interior of the very act of seeing.

On the story below, there is one room laid out in typical Japanese style, another room for administration purposes, a meeting room and a gymnasium. On the story that is on the same level as the point of access, right in front of the hallway and facing south, is the dining room. On the right are the kitchen and the sushi bar, and on the left there are guest rooms.

CAPISTRANO BEACH HOUSE

Architect: Rob Wellington Quigley
Location: Capistrano Beach, California, United States
Photographs: © Undine Pröhl

Circulation through the house is also full of contrasts in both the interior and exterior. Entrance on the east side is through two iron gates that lead to an intimate, formal vegetable garden enclosed by 6-foot (1.8-meter) high glass walls. A concrete pier crosses the sand to the porch and front door that face the cliffs and look on to the courtyard garden, perhaps the only suburban element in the whole design. The hall follows the curved glass wall and opens dramatically into the spacious living room, with its exposed roof beams and expansive view of the ocean. Along the beach side of the house is a small sitting room shaded by lattice work and a low-ceilinged dining room.

Quigley's designs have always been true to the reality in which they are placed—contextually, culturally, and climatically. The dramatic and exciting contrasts between the ocean and the land are interpreted architecturally: thick walls of poured concrete set off glass pavilions; deep shade and dappled light against the dazzling glare of the sand; exposed decks and terraces as opposed to quiet, private areas.

HOUSE AT CALELLA DE PALAFRUGELL

Architect: Josep Maria Bosch Reig, Lluís Jubert, and Eugènia Santacana
Location: Calella de Palafrugell, Spain
Photographs: © Eugeni Pons

The architect Josep Maria Bosch Reig built this house in 1965 as a weekend retreat for two families. Situated by the Mediterranean, just outside the town of Calella de Palafrugell on the Costa Brava, the house sits on a piece of land with a steep slope. The architect responded to the terrain by creating terraces at different levels, all with excellent views.

The renovation program carried out by the architects Lluis Jubert and Eugènia Santacana is an attempt to maintain the original style of the house and to modify the layout only where necessary, adapting it to the new needs of the two families.

This extremely comprehensive plan specifies a careful process for the interior renovation of an existing structure, to make the interior more habitable (quality of materials, organization and fluidity of spaces) as well as adding certain maritime touches.

SUMMER HOUSE

Architect: Philippe Meier
Location: Mies, Léman Lake, Switzerland
Photographs: © Jean-Daniel Pasquettaz

The Swiss architect Georges Addor built the original cabin in the 1950s. What makes the building interesting is the plasticity of the wood-work. Also, by experimenting with the asymmetry of the beams—one is mounted horizontally while the other tilts towards the floor—the architect made an otherwise uninteresting roof dynamic. Likewise, he included a brick fireplace to break up the interior geometry.

The new extension contains two bathrooms and dressing rooms, plus a large living room and kitchen with views of the lake and the surrounding landscape. The structural alterations are rooted in Addor's original designs, especially the plasticity of the new section.

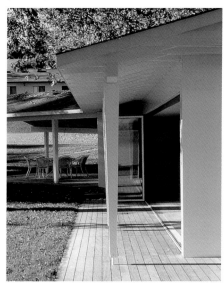